Happy Birthday to the best
    sister-in-law
        have!   —
            Jeanne
            1995

Thorns and Thrones

B. J. HOFF

Encouraging Words
for Faithful Living

Thorns
and
THRONES

B. J. HOFF

Book Design by Dianne Deckert
Artwork by Judy Hand
Calligraphy by Chris McGucken

WARNER
Press

Author's Acknowledgment

A special note of thanks to Cindy Maddox of Warner Press
who encouraged the idea and brought to the editing process
a unique gift of grace, excellence, and love.

Scriptures taken from the HOLY BIBLE: NEW INTERNATIONAL VERSION.
Copyright ©1973, 1978, 1984 by the International Bible Society.
Used by permission of Zondervan Bible Publishers.

All praise and thanks to
the One who wore the crown of thorns for you and me,
the One who was nailed to the Cross of Calvary,
the One who reigns as King of Kings eternally . . .
Jesus Christ, who is, and always will be, Lord.

TABLE OF CONTENTS

Thorns and THRONES

I'd rather gather roses without thorns, Lord,
   a bright and fragrant, beautiful bouquet
To decorate my world with pretty pleasures—
   the brambles and the briers, I'll throw away.

But you say I must pluck the thorns as well, Lord,
   although they'll pierce my heart and sting my soul;
You say that pain's a part of peace, you tell me
   that breaking is a part of being whole.

You say that if I truly want to know you,
   I must count everything but Christ a loss;
You ask me to exchange my way for yours, Lord,
   to trade contentment's kingdom for a cross.

And so I come before you, weak but willing;
   I seek to walk your path, and not my own;
I choose to share the crown of thorns you wore, Lord,
   until I kneel before your royal throne.

PEACE

eace is not a smooth, untroubled river
beneath a sunlit sky,
serene and warm . . .
The peaceful heart is like a trusting songbird
who clings to hope
and sings throughout the storm.

L*ORD* . . .

Your love is the branch of hope
  I cling to.
In the rising tide,
    in the restless wind,
        in the gathering storm,
            you are my peace.

 ou will keep in perfect peace
  him whose mind is steadfast,
because he trusts in you.

ISAIAH 26:3

IN THE HOLLOW OF HIS HAND

He leads me through the lifetime of my days.
He teaches me in countless little ways.
He guides me on so many paths unknown.
He guards me as a shepherd keeps his own.
He shields me, though I may not always see
The many ways my Lord delivers me.
He lifts me when I fall and helps me stand.
He holds me in the hollow of his hand.

DEAR LORD AND GUARDIAN OF MY SOUL...

Your Word is my counsel,
Your Power is my courage,
Your Promises, my comfort,
Your Presence, my confidence.
I rest my life,
My soul,
My future,
In your hands.

 e reached down from on high
and took hold of me.

PSALM 18:16

PEACE WITHIN HIS LOVE

Lord, still the clamor of our days
And calm our rushing, anxious ways;
In silence, teach us how to praise—
Give us peace within your love . . .

Lord, teach us true serenity,
The blessing of tranquility,
Let us find our deepest joy in Thee—
Give us peace within your love.

RINCE OF PEACE . . .

In the rush of the world around me,
  let me stand quietly in the shelter
    of your love . . .
Teach me to be more concerned
  about what I am than what I do,
    more inclined to pray than to push,
      and as eager to worship as I am to work . . .
Fill me, Lord,
  with peace at the very center of my soul
    in whatever circumstances I find myself . . .
Bless me, Lord,
  with the peace that comes from knowing
  I don't have to struggle to reach you,
  I don't have to succeed to please you—
  I don't have to do anything but belong to you
    and accept the love and the peace
      you want to give.

or he himself is our peace . . .
EPHESIANS 2:14

LET HIM LEAD

Secure in the promise
that God holds my hand,
I look to his leading each day . . .
Assured that he works
through all things for my best,
I follow, I trust, and I pray.

DIVINE COUNSELOR AND GUIDE . . .

When I falter in my faith,
 remind me to look up
  and reach out for your guiding hand.
When I hesitate to take the next step,
 give me a gentle nudge to get me going.
When I stop along the way,
 uncertain as to which road to take,
  teach me to wait until I clearly hear
   your firm, sure word of direction.
When shadows fall across my path
 and barriers block my journey,
  lead me by the light of your love
   on a steadfast way to your peace.

In your unfailing love you
will lead the people you have redeemed.

EXODUS 15:13

CONTENTMENT

Lord, grant us true contentment . . .
Acceptance of what each day brings,
Joy in you and not in things,
Tranquility in storm or strife,
Serenity in all of life;
That when you whisper, 'Peace, be still,'
We'll wait upon your perfect will,
Knowing we will soon be blessed
By love that only wants our best.
Help us see that we are meant
To rest in you . . . and be content.

LL-WISE AND LOVING FATHER . . .

Let us never forget
that in all things you send
   there is blessing.
Make us ever mindful
that every problem leading us to pray
   also leads us deeper into your presence,
and every trial
that takes us to our knees
   also brings us closer to your throne.
Let us always see
that every adversity
   is your opportunity,
every burden a chance
   to share your cross,
and that many times our tears
   most clearly reflect the vision of your grace.

have learned to be content
whatever the circumstances. . . .
I have learned the secret of being content
in any and every situation. . . . I can do everything
through him who gives me strength.

PHILIPPIANS 4:11-13

STILL WATERS

here's a time of still waters
that comes to us all,
a time when we hear
the Lord's soft, gentle call . . .
He asks us to trust him,
to be still and rest,
as he works to accomplish
his will for our best.

ESUS, TENDER SHEPHERD
OF MY SOUL . . .

This place to which you have brought me, Lord,
   was not of my own choosing.
You called me out from the rushing traffic,
away from the crowd and clamor,
away from the noise of getting things done,
accomplishing goals and achieving,
away from reaching and striving,
   into the quiet and peace of just . . . *being.*
You led me along a cool, grassy path
to a tranquil stream of clear water,
to rest and pray and listen and wait
   as you work your will in the silence.
How was I to know, dear Lord,
that in the simple act
of being still and trusting you
I was finally fulfilling your will?

e leads me beside quiet waters,
   he restores my soul.

PSALM 23:2, 3

THE QUIET HEART

The quiet heart finds blessing
in small gifts of gentle beauty,
assurance in warm, peaceful hours of rest.
The quiet heart finds joy
and true contentment always nearby,
for the quiet heart knows simple things are best.

ENTLE JESUS . . .

Let me take nothing for granted, Lord,
especially the small and simple things—
the pure and lovely, but often inconspicuous things.

Help me to see the splendor in a patch of wildflowers,
sense the mystery of a fog-curtained river at dawn,
admire the grace of a country lane,
and celebrate the glory of a rainbow.

Grant me a glimpse of your infinite care
in the pattern of an oak leaf,
a bee on a blossom, a mother bird,
a friend's smile.

Quiet my heart, Lord;
make me keenly aware
of the blessings of beauty all around me
and continually grateful for the confirmation
of your love in all of life.

e will quiet you with his love.

ZEPHANIAH 3:17

SONGS IN THE QUIET

Peace and warm contentment
flow from beauty to the heart—
When life brings quiet moments,
wait and rest . . .
Look closely at the lovely things
surrounding you each day,
And take joy from every gift
with which you're blessed.

 ONDERFUL GOD,
  MERCIFUL FATHER . . .

I thank you for the quiet times,
the blessed, peaceful, healing times
in which I can do nothing
but feel your presence.
I praise you for the gentle times,
the warm and silent, tranquil times
in which I lean entirely
on your love.

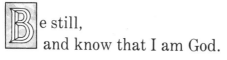 e still,
  and know that I am God.

PSALM 46:10

And we know that in all things
God works for the good
of those who love him.

ROMANS 8:28

GOD WITH US

He is the GOD OF OUR COMFORT,
Who vows to uphold and sustain;
He is the SHEPHERD who leads us
Through every dark valley of pain.
He is the LORD OF COMPASSION,
Who weeps with us, sharing our loss;
He is the MERCIFUL SAVIOR
Who purchased our peace on a cross.

OH, LORD, MY CONSOLATION AND MY REFUGE . . .

You are the center of my life, Lord . . .
Between me and every storm,
   every problem, every sorrow,
You stand firm and unchanging
   with your Word to give me strength,
   your presence to give me comfort,
   your touch to give me healing,
   your love to give me hope
      and make me whole.
You are my hiding place,
   my shelter, and my peace.

 You are my hiding place;
   you will protect me from trouble
and surround me with songs of deliverance.

PSALM 32:7

He is a shield to those
who take refuge in him.

PROVERBS 30:5

Thorns
of
Need

THRONE
of
Love

A FACE IN THE CROWD

"Who touched me?" asked the Master
    as he walked among the crowd.
Then he turned and saw a woman
    kneeling in the dust, head bowed.
His disciples were astonished—
    how could Jesus recognize
One brief touch from this small woman
    with the frightened, pleading eyes?
With great patience, he stood listening
    as she told of her disease;
Then he gently smiled and said,
    "My child, you're healed . . . now go in peace."
What a beautiful reminder
    that the Savior is aware
When a needy soul comes searching
    for his endless love and care.
Though the multitude may press him,
    we are blessed that God's own Son
Cares for every child as tenderly
    as if there were but one.

COMPASSIONATE SAVIOR . . .

We cannot hope to comprehend
your heart of love,
    your well of mercy,
        your continual awareness of our need.
We cannot begin to understand
how you hear the voices of millions—
each cry unique,
    a single sound
        recognized and identified by name.
But we believe and cling to the assurance
that we are your own,
    that we are known
        and loved and cherished
        heart by heart,
      soul by soul,
        one by one.

"You see the people crowding against you,"
his disciples answered, "and yet you can
ask, 'Who touched me?' " But Jesus kept
looking around to see who had done it.

MARK 5:31, 32

I love those who love me,
and those who seek me find me.

PROVERBS 8:17

NAME ABOVE ALL NAMES

He is HOPE for all the hopeless,
 The WAY for those who seek,
A LIGHT for those in darkness,
A HELPER for the weak.
He is FREEDOM for the prisoner,
A RANSOM for our shame,
He is SAVIOR, LORD, and MASTER—
JESUS is his name.

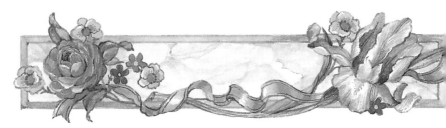

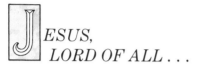

*J*ESUS,
    LORD OF ALL . . .

The fullness of the Father's love
    is contained in your blessed name.
You became like us
    that you might become for us
        the perfect sacrifice, the final peace,
            our Savior, Lord, and King eternal.
May our lives every day
    reflect your unconditional love,
        that others will be drawn
            to the abundant life you offer.
May we speak 'Jesus'
    to the world by acts of love.

 have come that they may have life,
and have it to the full.

JOHN 10:10

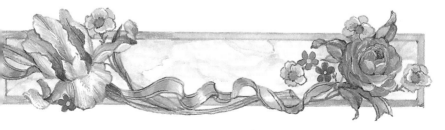

LANDSCAPES

The landscape of a day
is never barren . . .
Upon each hour is painted
at least one gift—
the sunrise of a smile,
the rainbow of a wish,
the gentle, peaceful sunset
of contentment—
God gives us beauty
for all our days
in small and unexpected ways
to bless the heart
and lift the spirit skyward.

OVING CREATOR . . .

Thank you
 for the everyday gifts of splendor
 I so often take for granted.
Remind me to open my eyes
 and see your divine touch
 in all things around me.
No matter where I am, Lord,
 make me daily aware
 of the breathtaking beauty,
 the glories of creation,
 that so wondrously proclaim
  your awesome power . . .
 yet so exquisitely and tenderly
  reflect your love.

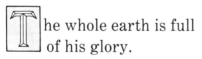
he whole earth is full
of his glory.

ISAIAH 6:3

I sing for joy
at the works of your hands.

PSALM 92:4

37

HIS LOVE

His love goes far beyond our dreams,
    beyond our aspirations.
His love surpasses all our plans,
    our hopes and expectations.
His love outreaches time and place
    and spans all generations.
His love outgives the greatest gifts—
    it knows no limitations.

OVING SAVIOR . . .

Too many times, Lord, when I see a dream die,
I allow disappointment to engulf me.
I lose hope because my plans have come to nothing,
and it's so much easier to give up
than try again.
Too many times, Lord, when it seems
that I'm only spinning my wheels
from one day to the next, year after year,
attaining nothing but age and bruises,
I want to drop out of the race
and bask in my failures.
But then you come and tap me gently
on the shoulder to remind me
that I wasn't made for success,
but for your glory;
that I wasn't called to win,
but simply to run;
and that your love is more than enough
through it all.

nd I pray that you, being rooted
and established in love,
may have power . . . to grasp how wide
and long and high and deep
is the love of Christ.

EPHESIANS 3:17, 18

MEETING GOD
IN THE HEART OF A FRIEND

The miracle of friendship
speaks from one heart to another,
listens for unspoken needs,
recognizes secret dreams,
understands the silent things
that only love can know. . .
God's precious gift of friendship
brings two lives, two souls together,
lets their spirits touch and meet,
teaches them to grow and reach,
helps them both to be the very best
that they can be.

 *RACIOUS LORD . . .*

So many times
  you have come to me
    through the kindness,
    the understanding,
    the caring heart
      of my faithful friend.
Time after time,
  you have revealed your love for me
    through her quick smile,
    her endless patience,
    her eagerness to share,
      to encourage, to comfort.
Thank you for her life, Lord,
  and her willingness to be a part of mine.
Touch her life through me,
  as you have blessed my life through her.

wo are better than one . . .
  If one falls down,
  his friend can help him up.

ECCLESIASTES 4:9, 10

41

OUR MORNING STAR

His love greets us every morning
with new blessings for the day;
with each sunrise, we embrace
the grace of God.
Ever mindful of his providence,
his never-failing care for us,
we celebrate the greatness
of our God.

L IGHT OF THE WORLD, BRIGHT MORNING STAR . . .

Your love is the sunrise
  that makes all our days new,
    that lights the soul
      and shines a beacon on tomorrow.
There is no darkness in the heart
  where your love lives, Lord,
    no shadows dimming the horizon of today
    or days to come.
Your grace and goodness, ever new,
  bring light and hope to all of life.
    We lift our hearts in thankful prayers
    and joyful praise.

H e is like the light of morning
  at sunrise.

2 SAMUEL 23:4

THE RANSOM

The Man
who upon the cross was nailed
looked down upon
a crowd in need
    who did not recognize their need . . .
a crowd in darkness
    who did not recognize the Light . . .
a crowd in chains
    who did not recognize their Deliverer . . .
And yet he stayed,
    a ransom
    paid in full
to purchase grace for the sinner,
freedom for the prisoner,
hope for the hopeless,
and life for the dying . . .
Behold—
    our substitute
    our sacrifice,
    our Savior.

AMB OF GOD . . .

Thank you
for your sacrificial love . . .
for standing in for me at Calvary,
taking my place,
erasing my sin,
redeeming my soul . . .
for paying the ransom I could never provide,
cancelling the debt I could never repay,
and reclaiming my soul for eternity
at the price of death on a cross . . .
Thank you, with all my heart,
for your saving love.

For this reason Christ is the mediator
of a new covenant, that those who are called
may receive the promised eternal inheritance—
now that he has died as a ransom to set them free.

HEBREWS 9:15

45

NEW EVERY MORNING

Oh, Lord, how you love
   to bless us.
   You stand waiting with the dawn
      of each new day with a fresh supply
         of goodness and gladness and grace
            for the hours to come.
   Your well of mercy is overflowing,
   Your store of blessings, inexhaustible.
   Sunrise to sunrise,
      season to season,
   Your love is unending and boundless.

UR LOVING LORD . . .

We need never run out of hope,
because you never run out of mercy.
What strength it gives,
what peace it lends
to know that whatever this day may hold
your promises stand,
unchanging and unfailing,
and however this day may end
your love will greet another sunrise.

his I call to mind
and therefore I have hope:
Because of the Lord's great love,
we are not consumed,
for his compassions never fail.
They are new every morning.

LAMENTATIONS 3:21-23

HEART OF LOVE

God's heart of love. . .
  Beats time in space,
Upholds the universe in place,
Gives rhythm to the flowing sea,
Composes nature's harmony,
Conducts the seasons' ebb and flow,
Directs the way the wind should blow,
Tunes morning song with evening rest,
Records the prayers of all the blessed,
Transposes darkest night to dawn,
As life and hope and joy sing on.

CREATOR GOD . . .
Your love was the prelude to my being,
   the breath that gave me life,
      the power that sustains me . . .
That you, on whose sovereign will
time itself depends and eternity hinges,
would form from dust and clay a living thing—
   a child of love,
      a child created in your image,
         a child on whom to lavish your affection
            and your goodness—
That you would name me as your Beloved
and bid me call you Father,
is more, infinitely more
than I can ever comprehend . . .
May every beat of my heart,
   every breath of my life,
      every part of all I am . . .
   reach far beyond and rise above
      the song of self
         to blend in harmony with the eternal *Gloria*
            all creation sings to you.

ou are worthy, our Lord and God,
   to receive glory and honor and power,
for you created all things,
and by your will they were created
and have their being.   *REVELATION 4:11*

Thorns
of
Uncertainty

THRONE
of
Faith

WALKING
IN THE
SHADOW OF THE SHEPHERD

There is nowhere we can go
    that he has not been there before us—
  We walk always in the shadow
    of his presence and his care . . .
For the Shepherd doesn't call his sheep
    to unfamiliar pasture—
He has promised that, where we are,
    we will also find him there.

ESUS, FAITHFUL SHEPHERD . . .

You know my resistance to change,
my determination to protect my comfort zone
from life's invasion.
You know that this new step I'm about to take
isn't something I *want* to do,
but rather something I *have* to do.
So today I'm remembering your past faithfulness, Lord—
the countless times you've led me through the shadows,
pulled me up a mountain, or carried me above a storm
to set me in a safe place.
Lead me again, Lord—
past my own reluctance and my stubbornness,
beyond my doubt and fear and apprehension.
Take my hand and lead me, Lord—
I'll follow.

e tends his flock like a shepherd:
He gathers the lambs in his arms
and carries them close to his heart.

ISAIAH 40:11

When he has brought out all his own,
he goes on ahead of them, and his sheep
follow him.

JOHN 10:4

HIS PLAN FOR ME

I see your hand, Lord,
In everything around me—
And in every aspect of my life,
I seek your will.
I see your plan, Lord,
In all the years behind me—
And in the days and years to come,
I'll trust you still.

WISE AND LOVING FATHER,
AUTHOR OF MY FAITH . . .

I lay before you
the life you gave to me.
Make me, Lord,
a pleasing child to Thee,
a special friend to Thee,
a source of delight to Thee . . .
Make me, Lord,
whatever you want me to be.

"**F**or I know the plans
I have for you," declares the Lord,
"plans to prosper you and not to harm you,
plans to give you hope and a future."

JEREMIAH 29:11

55

STEPPING-STONES

God makes stepping-stones
of all our days to guide us
on life's pathway . . .
When we would stand where we are,
in the safety of this hour,
He bids us move, step out, and follow him
to a new day . . .
Unknown, but not uncharted,
tomorrow waits for our arrival—
a day designed,
a place prepared with tender care
by the One who goes before us
to clear the road and light the way,
as with faith we walk behind him
in the footprints of his love.

JESUS,
MY EVER-PRESENT PILOT AND GUIDE . . .

Help me to begin each new day
with your name in my thoughts,
your love in my heart,
your Spirit at my side
to guide and lead me.
Help me, Lord, to celebrate in the quiet
the splendor of another sunrise,
to bow in thanksgiving
before the incredible beauty
of a clear blue sky,
and to stand in awe
as I add my voice of praise
to nature's chorus.
Every morning, Lord,
every precious day . . .
I will sing *Alleluia.*

he Lord delights in the way of the man
whose steps he has made firm;
though he stumble, he will not fall,
for the Lord upholds him with his hand.

PSALM 37:23

GOD'S SAFEKEEPING

e can rest within his care—
He doesn't slumber.
We can wait, for all his promises are true . . .
We can count on his safekeeping—
He's our Shepherd.
And what the Lord has promised, he will do.

 *OH, LORD, MY REFUGE,*
MY SAFEKEEPING . . .

In fear, you are my fortress.
In darkness, you are my light.
In doubt, you are my confidence.
In despair, you are my hope.
In weakness, you are my strength.
In the shelter of your love,
I am secure.
I rest my mind, my heart,
   my soul upon your care.

 eep me safe, O God,
for in you I take refuge.

PSALM 16:1

THROUGH ALL
LIFE'S CHANGING SEASONS

Life's seasons seem to change and flow so quickly—
One day we realize we're growing old;
The springtime of our years has long since faded,
And the summer sun has turned to autumn's gold.
We seem to feel life slipping through our fingers,
And we clutch each moment tightly till it's gone,
As if we could somehow hold on forever
And make this present joy shine on and on.
I'm grateful that my life was planned and fashioned
By a God of no beginning and no end,
A God to whom a lifetime is a brief touch,
No more than one soft whisper on the wind.
For this God, Lord of all life's changing seasons,
Lord of everything that's been and what will be,
Has promised me, when winter's finally over,
An endless spring in his eternity.

ORD OF MY LIFE,
LORD OF MY FOREVERS . . .

I thank you that I have this day to live.
I thank you for being a part
   of all my yesterdays,
And I thank you that you hold my tomorrows
   in your hand.
Life is a gift—
   and I celebrate it!
The future is yours—
   and I welcome it!

e has made everything beautiful
in its time. He has also set eternity
   in the hearts of men.

ECCLESIASTES 3:11

WHEN I AM WEAK

trength is often found
within the silence
while resting in the presence
of the Lord.
Abiding in his peace,
we feel his power;
while leaning on his love,
we are restored.

ROCK OF AGES . . .

When I am at my weakest point,
  you are just beginning.
When I know myself to be
  at the end of my strength,
I know my Lord to be
  at the front of the battle.
When I'm convinced
  I cannot go another step,
You sweep me into your mighty arms
    and carry me the rest of the way.
Lord, I abide in your marvelous grace.
I lean on your never-failing love.

y grace is sufficient for you,
  for my power is made perfect
  in weakness.

2 CORINTHIANS 12:9

Thorns
of
Suffering

THRONE
of
Hope

THE MASK OF PAIN

ain, you are a terrible deceiver . . .
   Parading yourself as an angry foe,
   pretending to be unyielding.
You shadow me, hound me, taunt me,
   as if by your mere presence
   you could conquer my spirit.
But I have learned to measure
   your ultimate strength,
   not by how much hurt you can inflict,
   but by how much of God's grace you call forth;
   not by how deeply you can wound,
   but by how frail you really are
   when put in perspective by his power . . .
And I have learned, at last,
   to believe that, even at your worst,
   you can never outlast a promise of God . . .
You can never outlive his love.

JESUS, MY DELIVERER, MY REFUGE . . .

When it seems that the pain
    will overwhelm me and send my spirit
        hurtling to the very edge of defeat,
            remind me of your presence—
                Help me stand . . .
Even when the hurting is greater
    than my hope, and suffering seems to be
        the very essence of my days,
            remind me of your promise—
                Help me stand . . .
In the power of your Word,
In the quiet of your Peace,
In the light of your Love—
        Help me stand.

When you pass through the waters,
    I will be with you;
    and when you pass through the rivers,
    they will not sweep over you.
    When you walk through the fire,
    you will not be burned . . .
    Do not be afraid, for I am with you.

ISAIAH 43:2, 5

SUNDAY'S COMING . . .

She kept her quiet vigil
  in the shadow of the cross,
A youthful, sad-eyed woman
    weeping softly for her loss . . .
    It was Friday . . . and her son was going to die . .

The infant she had cradled
  to her heart in other days
Looked down upon her anguish
    with compassion in his gaze . . .
    It was Friday . . . and her son was going to die . .

The toddler who had laughed
  and played beside her in the sun
Was suffering now before her eyes,
    and nothing could be done . . .
    It was Friday . . . and her son was going to die .

The young boy who had brought her
  so much joy throughout the years
Was dying as an outcast
    while she watched him through her tears . . .
    It was Friday . . . and her son was going to die .

The man who hung above her
   had done nothing wrong, she knew—
He'd been a loving son,
   a kind and gentle person, too . . .
      It was Friday . . . and her son was going to die . . .

Her mother's heart was shattered,
   but she managed to forgive—
For she had the Father's word
   that in three days her son would live . . .
      Sunday's coming . . . and the Son is going to rise . . .

ON OF THE FATHER . . .

   Let us never forget
      that after every Friday of sorrow
         comes your promised Sunday of joy.
   Praise the Lord—
   for the Son is truly risen!

n the third day
he will rise again.

LUKE 18:33

HIS LOVE SHINES ON

His love shines on . . .
   Beyond time's distant, vast horizon,
Past yesterday, today,
   and each tomorrow . . .
Though joy grows dim
And sunlight fades to shadow,
His love shines on in our hearts,
   beyond our sorrow.

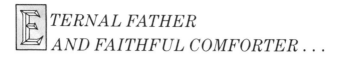

ETERNAL FATHER AND FAITHFUL COMFORTER...

Even with the shadow of the cross
ever before you,
you managed to look beyond
the darkness of Calvary
to the sun of eternity.
Help me, Lord,
as I walk through this wilderness
of loneliness and loss,
to look beyond the desolation
of my cross and keep my eyes
on the Son of eternity.

ven the darkness will not be dark
to you; the night will shine like the day,
for darkness is as light to you.

PSALM 139:12

THE THIRD CROSS

Two crosses stood upon a hill
 Where soon a third was raised.
Two criminals awaiting death
Looked toward the third, amazed
To see who hung between them,
Suffering quietly as he died—
The gentle son of Joseph—
Why would *he* be crucified?
And still across the centuries,
The question sounds today:
Why would the gentle Son of God
Meet death in such a way?
If die he must, why not a death
Of honor and acclaim—
Why choose to be identified
With sinners and their shame?
And yet his death upon the cross
Enables us to see—
He comes to us right where we are,
Not where we'd like to be.
Amidst our darkness and disgrace,
Our suffering and our sin,
The Savior comes to each of us,
Time and time again.

AMB OF GOD . . .

Sometimes we look for you in lofty places,
  when all the time you stand among us,
    coming to meet us at the place of our need.
In the midst of our failure, our sin and shame,
  there you are, with outstretched hands,
    quietly waiting, gently saying,
      "Here I am . . . come as you are . . .
      Come to me . . ."

here they crucified him,
  along with the criminals—
one on his right, the other on his left.

LUKE 23:33

But God demonstrates his own love for us
in this: While we were still sinners,
Christ died for us.

ROMANS 5:8

GOD, OUR GOD

The God who takes a summer storm
 and ends it with a rainbow,
   who lights the very darkest night
   with silver stars above . . .
The God who, with a tiny seed,
 can form a perfect rosebud,
   is our God, and the One who heals
   our sorrow with his love.

LORD GOD . . .

I know you care about my sorrow;
I know you share the aching of my heart;
you taste my tears, you hold my hand.
My comfort, as I wait upon your peace,
is knowing that you are in this moment
with me, leading me and loving me
through it all.
My strength, as I rest within your presence,
is knowing that my God is
the God who creates,
the God who saves,
the God who heals,
the only God, the one God,
who never fails.

ou removed my sackcloth
and clothed me with joy . . .
O Lord my God,
I will give you thanks forever.

PSALM 30:11, 12

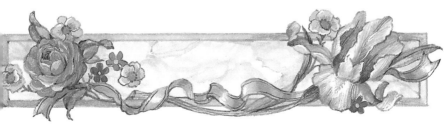

ONE HAND ON THE STARS

ow do we count the lives she touched,
The light she shed for years?
How do we see the difference she made
When we're looking through our tears?
How do we know the things that are
That never would have been
Without her valiant heart that dared
To fight, and fight again?
How do we know what flowers will bloom
From seeds of yesterday,
What songs are sung and dreams begun
Because she passed this way?
How do we measure the shining place
That time can never pale
In all the hearts that cheered her on
And willed her to prevail?
How did her spirit soar beyond
The suffering and the scars
To live with one hand clutching hope
And the other on the stars?
We may not know what she left behind
On the difficult path she trod . . .
But we know this much: her life's brief touch
Was from the hand of God.

In memory of Janet A. Winegardner 1961—1987

FATHER OF MERCY . . .

We cannot always understand
why you do not heal . . .
 why you do not raise our loved ones
  out of their suffering into wholeness and health.
But we can cling to this:
 you care for us,
 you grieve with us,
 you hold our hand,
 you dry our tears,
 and you give to us the assurance
  that every life counts,
  no matter how brief or gentle its whisper,
 and that beyond today, in your tomorrow,
  our loved ones have been healed and raised
   to live in health and eternal happiness
    with you.

Those who are wise will shine like the
brightness of the heavens, and those who lead
many to righteousness, like the stars for ever
and ever.

DANIEL 12:3

FROM GOD TO US

od gives us STRENGTH
    that we may be *Servants,*
God gives us HOPE
    that we may be *Encouragers,*
God gives us COMPASSION
    that we may be *Comforters,*
God gives us JESUS
    that we may be *Family.*

ATHER GOD . . .

As I go to share the pain
of this one you have placed upon my heart,
I ask you to send me
with the love of Jesus.
My own human nature would flee
from her suffering
or, even worse, attempt to offer
a fast fix, a quick cure.
Take me beyond that, Lord—
beyond my own weakness
and past the outer surface of her need
to the inner place of her silent cry for help.
Take me close enough
that my heart will ache with hers,
even break with hers;
close enough to light one small flame of hope
in the darkness of her despair;
close enough to touch her wound
with the balm of your healing;
close enough to give her a gift
of your love.

erve one another in love. . . .
Carry each other's burdens.

GALATIANS 5:13, 6:2

WHEN THERE ARE NO ANSWERS

Life will bring us questions without answers;
   To live is to encounter
   silent seasons of the soul,
When every prayer will seem to go unanswered
As we face events beyond
   our understanding or control.
Yet in the quiet darkness, Christ is working.
His silence in the shadows
   doesn't mean he doesn't care;
A part of faith is trusting without reason,
Believing, when he can't be seen
   or heard, that he's still there.
So when answers fail to come, don't be discouraged.
Keep leaning on his steadfast love
   and trusting in his will,
For knowing *why* won't really make a difference—
But growing close and knowing Jesus *will*.

ORD OF LIFE . . .

Teach me to wait patiently
  in the silence . . .
    To trust your guiding hand,
      your perfect will, your steadfast love
        even when I'm feeling most alone.
Teach me to ask, not *why,*
  but *what* . . .
    What do you want me to learn
    from this, Lord . . .
      what does it mean to my walk with you,
        in my relationship with you and others?
Let me seek, more than reasons, your wisdom,
  More than answers, your approval,
      More than your peace, your blessed presence
        in my life.

hen you will call, and the Lord
will answer; you will cry for help,
and he will say: Here am I.

ISAIAH 58:9

NO SHORTCUTS

He offers solid food to fill the spirit,
But in our rash impatience to be fed,
We glut ourselves with quick and easy junk food
Instead of reaching for the Living Bread.

He opens up his arms and bids us bring him
Our burdens, our discouragements and cares,
But we turn on a television preacher
In search of instant answers to our prayers.

He bids us to explore his Word, to study,
To learn about his nature and his way,
But that takes years of discipline and patience—
So we settle for a Scripture-verse-a-day.

He asks us to take up his cross and follow,
To share his sufferings and endure his trials,
But we look for another road to glory—
A smoother, wider road with fewer miles.

He does not promise health and wealth and sunshine
Or pain-free wish fulfillment to the blessed—
But he does say he will shelter and sustain us,
So that even in our struggles, we can rest. . .

Our human nature always seeks the shortcut,
The fastest route to where we want to be—
But God says, "Choose: happiness or holiness—
There is no easy road to Calvary."

 EAD ME, LORD . . .
    You are the Way,
        the one and only Way,
            and I choose to walk with you
                on the life-long journey
                    to wholeness . . . and holiness.
        Lord, give me strength for the journey.

 irect me in the path
        of your commands, for there I find delight.
Turn my heart toward your statutes
and not toward selfish gain.
Turn my eyes away from worthless things.

PSALM 119:35-37

He satisfies my desires
with good things.

PSALM 103:5

85

GOD'S YES

ow many are the promises
    that God has given us,
How great the confidence
    with which we're blessed:
That we are his beloved,
    cherished children of his heart,
Inheritors of all our Father's best.
He has pledged to us a love
    we can't begin to comprehend,
A love fulfilled and sealed by sacrifice;
He sent his only son
       as confirmation of that love—
God's every promise finds its *Yes* in Christ.

 LESSED LORD, OUR HOPE, OUR PEACE ...

> We ask
>   and we ask
>   and we ask
> for this and that,
> for more and more,
> for peace and painless living,
> for solutions to our problems,
> healing for our suffering,
> cessation of our grief,
> shelter, security, and safekeeping.
> How long, dear Lord; how long
>   before we see YOU, not your gifts,
>   YOU, not your blessings,
>   as the Answer,
>   the Solution,
>   the Fulfillment.
> How long before we recognize
>   the sufficiency of YOU?

 or no matter how many promises God has made, they are "Yes" in Christ.

2 CORINTHIANS 1:20

THE LEGACY

We have been given all things from above,
 A legacy gained from a treasury of love.
Endowed by a King who owns heaven and earth,
Yet sees us as precious, of infinite worth.
Rich beyond measure, we daily receive
Every blessing of goodness his love can conceive.
Though the Giver asks nothing of us, still we yearn
To bring something of value to him in return.
But what could we give him for all that he's done?
He has given us everything, even his Son.
Perhaps if we asked him how best to convey
Our thanksgiving, he'd smile and then quietly say,
"There's *one* thing I ask my children to do:
Love one another as I have loved you."

DEAR LORD AND FATHER . . .

As your love looks upon us
with the acceptance and forgiveness
of the redeeming Christ,
so let us look at one another
through your eyes
and see each other as you see us:
    Your Church
      Your Family
        Your Beloved.
Teach us, Lord, to love
as you love . . .
    Freely
      Fully
        Unselfishly
          Unconditionally.
Fill us with the love of Christ
and make us one in you.

Dear friends, since God so loved us, we also
ought to love one another. No one has ever
seen God; but if we love each other, God
lives in us and his love is made complete
in us.

1 JOHN 4:11, 12

SOLITUDE

The way to God
is through the desert—
no trumpets, no choirs
to herald his presence
or amplify my praise.
No telephone, no friends,
to distract me
from my emptiness.
No plans, no dreams,
to divert me
from my nothingness.
No ministry, no work
to delude me with the lie
of usefulness.
Nothing
but this season
in the desert
alone with God—
the only sounds
a proud heart breaking
and the quiet weeping
of one at last confronted
with the truth . . .
that my only self is sinful,
my only hope is mercy,
my only gift is salvation,
my only life is Christ.

 IVINE MASTER, HOLY GOD . . .

I come to meet you
   just as I am,
      bereft of all the things
         I once believed made me a person
         of value.
In the silence of solitude,
   in the desert place of my everydays
      where I come to seek your presence,
   you have taught me that my life
      is changed only by meeting you,
         that my life has meaning
         and value and beauty
            only when fully surrendered
         to you.

 ome near to God
and he will come near to you.

JAMES 4:8

Whoever finds his life
will lose it, and whoever loses his life
for my sake will find it.

MATTHEW 10:39

ALTARS

He doesn't wait for us to come
And meet him at his royal throne—
He comes to us as a loving father,
Reaching out to seek his own.

He doesn't ask for an unstained life
Or a past completely cleansed of sin—
He meets us where we are, no matter
What we've done or where we've been.

He breaks through all our old ideas
Of where to seek his dwelling place
And comes directly to our hearts
With healing love and saving grace.

He has no need for graven altars,
Vast cathedrals or crowded pews—
The sanctuary he loves best
Is a surrendered heart that he can use.

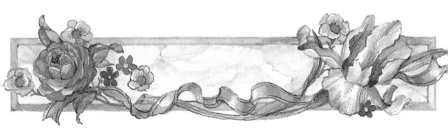

JESUS, MY SAVIOR,
FRIEND, AND MEDIATOR...

> You came to me
> behind the closed doors
> of my sin, my doubt,
>   and my confusion
> to open my heart,
> to free my soul,
> to prepare my spirit
>   for your indwelling.
> I come to you
> with the gift of myself—
> an offering of love—
> a life made new,
> a heart made clean,
> a will surrendered.
> For now and forever,
>   I am yours, my Lord.

he sacrifices of God are a broken spirit;
a broken and contrite heart.

PSALM 51:17

Let us then approach the throne of grace
with confidence, so that we may receive mercy
and find grace.

HEBREWS 4:16

THE FATHER'S QUESTION

What have you done in my name today, child. . .
  Who have you sheltered or fed?
How many lives have been warmed by my touch
  through something you've done or said?
How many, burdened by doubt and despair
  as they struggle through trouble and strife,
Gained courage and hope as you openly spoke
  of the way to a new, better life?
How many lonely hearts, searching for love,
  found their emptiness filled when you shared?
How many suffering found comfort and peace
  in the knowledge that somebody cared?
How many souls did you save from destruction
  by leading them into my light?
How many wrongs did you try to prevent
  by taking a stand for what's right?
Be mindful that when you love others, my child,
  you're showing your love for me, too . . .
Now, I ask you once more what you've done in my name—
  and how much are you willing to do?

FATHER OF US ALL . . .

Just as I am blessed by any act of love
done for one of my children,
I believe you are blessed when your children
show their love for one another.
And just as I am grieved when one of my children
is victimized by rejection or cruelty or indifference,
I know that you are grieved when your children
cause one another pain.
Let me never forget that when I ignore another's need,
I ignore you.
When I reject an opportunity to love, I reject you.
Lord, enable me and empower me with a love
that is willing to approach the unapproachable,
to touch the untouchable, to love the unlovable,
to accomplish the impossible in your name . . .
with your love.

For I was hungry and you gave me something to eat,
I was thirsty and you gave me something to drink,
I was a stranger and you invited me in,
I needed clothes and you clothed me,
I was sick and you looked after me,
I was in prison and you came to visit me . . .
Whatever you did for one of the least of these . . .
you did for me.

MATTHEW 25:35, 36, 40

"The best rose-bush, after all,
is not that which has the fewest thorns,
but that which bears the finest roses."
HENRY VAN DYKE